# Amazing Pictures and Facts About Dublin

By: Mina Kelly

# Introduction

Dublin is a very old city, which, though it is a fully fledged modern city, still retains some of its traditions and beauty. Let's explore Dublin!

# Where is Dublin?

Dublin is the capital city of Ireland, a country off the European mainland. The city lies on the eastern shore of the Irish Sea, to the northwest of England.

# How Old is the City of Dublin?

Dublin celebrated its 'official' millennium in 1988, which means that the Irish government has recognized 988 AD as the year in which the city was settled. This settlement would later became the city of Dublin.

# What is the Population of Dublin?

The population of the city has been estimated to be about 535,000 people. If one includes the entire metropolitan area in this estimate, the number rises to about 1.8 million. All in all, it has a pretty low population compared to other major cities.

# What is the Weather Like in the City?

Similar to much of northwestern Europe, Dublin experiences a maritime climate, with cool summers, mild winters, and a lack of temperature extremes. The average maximum January temperature is 48 °F, while the average maximum July temperature is 68 °F. On average, the sunniest months are May and June, and the wettest month is October - however, Dublin's sheltered location on the east coast makes it the driest place in Ireland, so it receives only about half the rainfall of the west coast.

# What is the Landscape Like Around the City?

Dublin is located at the mouth of the River Liffey, and is bordered by a low mountain range to the south and surrounded by flat farmland to the north and west. The Liffey divides the city in two between the Northside and the Southside. Each of these is further divided by two lesser rivers – the River Tolka Running southeast into Dublin Bay, and the River Dodder running northeast to the mouth of the Liffey. There are many more bodies of water throughout the city.

# What Languages are Spoken in Dublin?

The main language spoken in Dublin is English. The traditional language of the country is Gaelic, and so on public/official buildings names are written in both languages, but rarely do you hear anybody actually speaking Gaelic.

# What is the Currency Used in Dublin?

Ireland is a part of the European Union, which all uses the same currency, the euro. One dollar in the United States is about the same as 0.96 euros!

# How Big is the City?

The city has an area of 44.5 square miles. It is not a very big city in terms of area, especially compared to other major cities around the world - it does not even make any lists!

# What Are the Origins of the Name of the City?

The name of the city comes from the Gaelic words *Dubh* and *Linn*, which translates to "Black Pool." It also comes from the name *Baile Atha Cliath*, which means "Ford of the Reed Hurdles."

# Are There Many Young People Living in Dublin?

This city is full of young people. It has been estimated that about fifty percent of the city's residents are under the age of 25!

# Are There Many Pubs in Dublin?

Dublin is famous for its pubs, of which there are over 1,000 in the city. The oldest pub in Ireland is also here, called the Brazen Head - there has been a pub in that spot since 1198!

# Have Any Famous People Come From Dublin?

Many famous writers have gone to Trinity College in Dublin. A few of the most well known are Oscar Wilde, Jonathan Swift, and Bram Stoker (the creator of Dracula).

# What is One of the Most Popular Methods of Transportation?

The most popular method of transportation is by bike. There are over 120 miles of bike trails throughout the city, with 450 public bikes at 40 different bike stations!

# What Famous Person is Buried Here?

Everyone has heard of Valentine's Day, but did you know that this holiday is based off of a real person, St. Valentine? He was killed for marrying people in ancient times, and so has become the basis for the holiday of love. He is buried in Dublin, in Whitefriar Street Church!

# Are There Parks in the City?

There are many parks in the city, the most famous of which is Phoenix Park. This park is five times bigger than Hyde Park in England, and two times as big as Central Park in America. The park stretches over 1,750 acres of land, and even has the Dublin Zoo inside of it!

# Is Taxi Driving a Popular Profession?

Taxi driving is a popular profession because the pay is very good. On average, a taxi driver makes four times as much money as about 96 percent of his or her clients!

# What Famous Song was First Played in Dublin?

Have you ever heard the famous classical score, Handel's *Messiah?* This beautiful piece was first played to an audience of 700 people in the Temple Bar, on April 13th, 1742. Now, it is performed every year on Fishamble Street.

# What is One of the Iconic Parts of the City?

One of the things that the city is known for is its O'Connell Bridge, built in 1863. This bridge is famous for its dimensions - it is as long as it is wide! It is the only bridge like this in the world!

# Are There Any Other Cities Named After Dublin?

There are many cities around the world that have been named after Dublin. In the United States, there are twelve places named Dublin, and in Australia there are six!

# Do Many People Visit Dublin Each Year?

Every year, anywhere from 6 to 7 million people make a visit to the city of Dublin. This is a pretty big increase from only ten years ago, and the numbers only get higher and higher!

Made in the USA
Middletown, DE
09 March 2018